BEWARE OF
SEDUCING SPIRITS

Mark T. Barclay

All scripture references are quoted from the
King James Version of the Holy Bible
unless otherwise noted.

Scripture quotations marked "NIV" are taken from the
Holy Bible, New International Version®, NIV®, copyright © 1973,
1978, 1984, International Bible Society, Zondervan.
Used by permission. All rights reserved.

Scripture quotations marked "TLB" are taken from
The Living Bible copyright © 1971. Used by permission of Tyndale
House Publishers, Inc., Wheaton, IL 60189. All rights reserved.

Second Edition
Third Printing 2011

ISBN-10: 0-944802-25-7
ISBN-13: 978-0-944802-25-0

Mark Barclay Ministries
2010 North Stark Road, Midland, MI 48642-9439
www.marktbarclay.com

CONTENTS

INTRODUCTION

Believe me, folks, as you read this book, many things will go through your mind. Some of you will think of yourselves and how these seducing spirits have tried to minister to you. Others will think of friends and family members who once served the Lord so well and fervently but now have been turned over to gossip, talebearing, malice, strife, and jealousy and are always accusing the church leaders.

Please beware! Let this book be a warning to you. I pray that the devil and demons will be exposed through this writing.

There really are seducing, deceiving spirits roaming the earth wanting to minister to you. Don't let the religion and pride of Saul get on you. Don't let the uprising and insolent spirit of Korah get on you. Don't let the hatred and seduction of Jezebel work against your leaders. Don't let the jealous conspiracy spirit of Absalom get on you. Shake them off and commune only with the Holy Spirit.

I hope you will enjoy this book. I have spent many hours meditating and searching out the truths that you'll find on these pages. I have combined my study notes with the administrative notes I have kept through the years serving as a pastor.

I must say that I have personally encountered each of these spirits as I have dealt with leaders and members of local churches. Though I've found that the name and blood of Jesus are most sovereign, it surprises me that so many people cannot be helped because they give in to demonic seduction.

I pray this book will be a great strength to your life and ministry in Christ. I write it by my own hand in obedience to the Lord Jesus. Let these words run around in your heart and either be a warning to you or set you free.

A WORD FROM THE AUTHOR

The heart of the author is one of humility, yet the presentation herein is quite bold. It is not the intention of the author to hurt anyone in any way with this writing but to stir up those who have been attacked by these spirits so they can free themselves.

Not one person anywhere in the Body of Christ has to give heed to these spirits or their style of life. No—not one!

The author plans to warn some readers, inform others, and even set some free.

This book is by far best read if one is like Jesus—humble, holy, and not a reviler.

This is not a book on demonology.

It is a book about people who are close to being in trouble with God because of demon activity or fleshly bad attitudes.

CHAPTER 1
THE DEVIL'S SLY TECHNIQUES

"Now the Spirit speaketh expressly, that in the latter times some shall depart from the faith, giving heed to seducing spirits, and doctrines of devils;

Speaking lies in hypocrisy; having their conscience seared with a hot iron . . ."

1 Timothy 4:1-2

Listen, my friend, before you read any further into this book, look at what verse 6 of this same chapter says. Many people say, "Let's talk about all positive things; let's not talk about [face] our problems. Let's not listen to any preacher who is being at all negative or corrective." It's sad to say, but many people only want their fancy tickled or their itchy ears scratched. I've quoted verse 6 below:

"If thou put the brethren in remembrance of these things, thou shalt be a good minister of Jesus Christ, nourished up in words of faith and of good doctrine, whereunto thou hast attained."

1 Timothy 4:6

Did you read that carefully? Did you pick out what the Holy Spirit is saying? He said I was a good minister of Jesus Christ. That's right. Because I will deal with the

1

brethren and remind you about these seducing spirits and those who listen to them, I am considered by God to be a good minister. Praise God! He also says that my doctrine is good and I have been nourished up in the words of faith. Actually, we all know this isn't Brother Barclay's scripture, but it refers to any minister who deals with God's people according to these scriptures.

Regarding the devil's trickery and schemes, the first verse we read was dealing with seduction. Some versions use the word deception. Either way, you are in trouble if you give in to these voices.

The devil has always had a plan to hurt and demobilize God's people. He will use anything or anyone he can. For example, just before God began to restore some true Joshuas and Calebs to our modern-day pulpits, the devil totally influenced a preacher who drew people away to South America, and it turned out to be a big scandal. The whole body of Christ made the thing famous through their fear. That's right! Nowadays, years later, people yell "cult" at every preacher around who walks in authority. Even so, God moves on with His remnant, and pastoral-ruled church government has seized almost all of the independent churches as well as a large portion of the others. Somehow God always gets His way. Thank Him for it!

The word "cult" is a very well-spread, commonly-used word among Christian and religious people. The problem, however, is that most people who are yelling "cult" or "cultish" don't have the slightest idea what it means. It just seems to be the popular slang word of the hour. (The teens have their slang, the street has its slang, and the Church has theirs.)

It does not surprise me that the devil has recently stuck his head up again to pollute, slander, and defame. God's people are about to enter into the greatest, most awesome revival that has ever touched planet earth. That's right! It's going to happen in the midst of the local church. We are going to enjoy a great fear of God, and we'll begin to show a real reverence for His holy presence. (I suppose there will be enough rebels and pretenders that we will also get to see the fireworks of God's judgment as well.) Don't you see what's been happening? The devil has already made some of his best preventive moves against this revival. He has really produced another masterpiece that will once again thrust fear into the midst of God's people. The result: A people that will be overly cautious and suspicious of preachers, teachers, and church leaders. It's a shame that so many Christians listen to him (the devil). This is the hour for us to grow deep roots in our local churches and put trust in our leaders. So what happens? The devil drags out all the sin, sadness, and shame that he can about every preacher he can find.

Also, in the midst of this, the gospel publishing market is flooded with all kinds of literature and printed material warning us to beware of the preachers and teachers. What a slick move for the devil. I wonder why so many Christians consistently fall for his trickery. Listen, friends, in the day you need your leaders the most, satan is polluting your minds about their integrity by causing you to look at and wrestle with their flesh and blood (men). Don't Christians know better than this? We read in the Bible already that we are being warned to watch out for seducing spirits—not preachers. Now listen, I know we should be wise and alerted to false prophets and teachers who will be piled up by those who only want to hear what they desire (read 2 Tim. 4:3-4). Even so, we must learn to look through the eyes of the Holy Spirit and be led by Him.

Most Christians do not try the spirits. Instead, they put the preacher on trial. They have a trial and rip apart a man's life, ministry, family, and reputation just to bring indictment against him. Do you know how people judge a minister? By his fruit? They say they do, but really they don't. Most of them do not really care about his longevity or his productivity. The way modern Christians judge leaders is by their belongings. They don't know them by their fruit or by their spirit but by the car they drive, home they own, ring they are wearing, or clothes they have. Come on, folks! You and I know that it's wrong to judge this way. Not only is it wrong to judge this way, but the whole perspective has shifted from demon activity to preacher activity. How sad. I wonder how the Lord puts up with such immaturity. You know, don't you, that the devil and his demons love Christians to be this way? Sure they do. While Christians are watching all the smut and slander reports about different ministers, the devil is gardening in their backyard.

Let me remind you, believer, that the preacher is not your enemy or your problem. Your problem and your enemy is satan—the accuser of the brethren and the father of lies. The scripture I quoted at the beginning of this chapter told about seducing spirits, not seducing people. The person you need to be worried about is you. The Bible says here that these seducing spirits will cause some to depart (purposely abandon) the faith. "The faith" here is in reference to Christianity, not the "faith movement," as we call it today. It's sad, isn't it, that some people will give heed to these spirits? It will cost them everything.

There is another scripture that fits in here real well. It

is found in Ephesians, chapter 6, verses 10-12. Here is what it says:

> *"Finally, my brethren, be strong in the Lord, and in the power of his might.*
>
> *Put on the whole armour of God, that ye may be able to stand against the wiles of the devil.*
>
> *For we wrestle not against flesh and blood, but against principalities, against powers, against the rulers of the darkness of this world, against spiritual wickedness in high places."*
>
> Ephesians 6:10-12

Can you see it? Were you reminded of it? We are not to wrestle with people but with the dirty, dark spirits that live in the atmosphere of our earth. Listen! The devil is counting on the fact that you will do what so many others do. They look at mere men and ignore the real enemy. You are not in a carnal, natural war, folks. You are in a very strategic, spiritual one. Keep your eyes off the preachers, and put them on the Lord Jesus Christ. Remember, don't be wrestling with anyone but your adversary, the devil. Be sober.

> *"Be sober, be vigilant; because your adversary the devil, as a roaring lion, walketh about, seeking whom he may devour . . ."*
>
> 1 Peter 5:8

Your mind is in the arena of life that the devil wants to penetrate. He wants to shoot burning, fiery darts into your thinking processes and hinder and pervert your communication with God and the brethren. The devil wants you to be in strife because that is where he operates best. He wants you to think and live impurely. He wants you to give up and go shipwreck. The devil wants you to talk against and take bad actions against your spiritual leaders. Listen, friend, the devil wants to seduce you and pervert you and deceive you. Watch out for him. Don't let him do it. Be pure, be spiritual, act uprightly, and follow Bible standards and guidelines in your life. You won't be sorry—no, not ever!

Check out the following scriptures and meditate on them:

> *"But if ye have bitter envying and strife in your hearts, glory not, and lie not against the truth.*
>
> *This wisdom descendeth not from above, but is earthly, sensual, devilish.*
>
> *For where envying and strife is, there is confusion and every evil work."*

James 3:14-16

> *"Above all, taking the shield of faith, wherewith ye shall be able to quench all the fiery darts of the wicked."*

Ephesians 6:16

> *"Put on the whole armour of God, that ye may be able to stand against the wiles of the devil."*

Ephesians 6:11

> *"Unto the pure all things are pure: but unto them that are defiled and unbelieving is nothing pure; but even their mind and conscience is defiled."*

Titus 1:15

> *"Why do ye not understand my speech? even because ye cannot hear my word.*

Ye are of your father the devil, and the lusts of your father ye will do . . . for he is a liar, and the father of it."

John 8:43-44

". . . for the accuser of our brethren is cast down, which accused them before our God day and night."

Revelation 12:10

CHAPTER 2
THE SPIRIT OF KORAH

"The Uprising and Insolent Spirit"

Numbers 16:1-50

> *"Korah, son of Izhar . . . became insolent*
>
> *and rose up against Moses. With them were 250 Israelite men, well-known community leaders who had been appointed members of the council.*
>
> *They came as a group to oppose Moses and Aaron and said to them, 'You have gone too far! The whole community is holy, every one of them, and the LORD is with them. Why then do you set yourselves above the LORD's assembly?'"*
>
> Numbers 16:1-3 (NIV)
>
> *"Moses also said to Korah, 'Now listen, you Levites!*
>
> *Isn't it enough for you that the God of Israel has separated you from the rest of the Israelite community and brought you near himself to do the work at the LORD's tabernacle and to stand before the community and minister to them?*
>
> *He has brought you and all your fellow Levites near himself, but now you are trying to get the priesthood too.*

*It is against the LORD that you and all your followers
have banded together . . ."*

Numbers 16:8-11 (NIV)

"Then the LORD said to Moses,

*'Say to the assembly, 'Move away from the tents of
Korah . . .'"*

Numbers 16:23-24 (NIV)

*"Then Moses said, 'This is how you will know that
the LORD has sent me to do all these things and that it
was not my idea:*

*If these men die a natural death and experience only
what usually happens to men, then the LORD has not
sent me.*

*But if the LORD brings about something totally
new . . ."*

Numbers 16:28-30 (NIV)

*"And fire came out from the LORD and consumed the
250 men who were offering the incense."*

Numbers 16:35 (NIV)

*"The next day the whole Israelite community grum-
bled against Moses and Aaron. 'You have killed the
LORD's people,' they said."*

Numbers 16:41 (NIV)

*"But when the assembly gathered in opposition to
Moses and Aaron and turned toward the Tent of
Meeting, suddenly the cloud covered it and the glory
of the LORD appeared.*

*Then Moses and Aaron went to the front of the Tent of
Meeting,*

and the LORD *said to Moses,*

*'Get away from this assembly so I can put an end to
them at once.' And they fell facedown."*

Numbers 16:42-45 (NIV)

These have to be some of the most powerful verses in
the Bible. They are so revealing and remind us of the awe-
someness of God. What did you feel when you read these
scriptures? Did it remind you of anything that's happening
today? When I read this whole chapter, I was really
reminded of how people were back then—and how they
still remain the same today. It's really something that all
these years have slipped by, and yet humanity has improved
so little.

When I meditated in this chapter of the Bible, it caused
me to look more closely at so many of our churches today.
Both denominational and independent churches have
plenty of people like Korah and his band of men. I have
been in enough church business meetings and board meetings to know they resemble this Bible account of Korah. I
wonder if some church people read this Korah account and
then set out in their churches to duplicate it. It has been a
very familiar spirit in the recent years. I hope you never get
caught up in it!

Let's look a little closer to see what we can learn about
these things. Let me draw your attention back to verses 1
and 2. I really like the word used in the New International
Version—insolent. Webster's Dictionary defines this word
as one who is boldly disrespectful in speech or behavior,
impertinent, arrogantly contemptuous, overbearing. There
are many Christians today who seem to fit this description.

Korah became insolent and rose up against Moses. This

is what always happens when people get insolent. They always rise against leaders. No one loved these people more than their pastor, Moses, and his right-hand man, Aaron. In fact, if Moses and Aaron wouldn't have prayed for them so consistently, they would have been wiped out several times—by God Himself. Even so, they turned against Moses and rose up against him with Korah as their leader.

Why is it that everyone who gets into trouble in their own heart has to blame the pastor or the church? Will there ever be a time when rebellious, insolent people will take accountability for their own sadness and actions?

Look even closer now and see who Korah got to side with him. It wasn't the poor, weak little lambs. It was the leaders—250 well-known church leaders. But that is not all. They were also appointees and members of the council.

Just like today, huh? If one Korah in the midst of hundreds of people becomes insolent and mouthy, many of the other leaders join in on the uprisal. Sheep do not do such things!

Why is it this way? Why can't these people just leave peacefully with their belligerent hearts? What possesses these people to cause trouble and collect a band of people with "like precious trash" in their hearts? Why be a carnal trash collector?

Would your friends call you by your real name and say sweet, holy things about you, or would you be one they would call Sister Smut or Brother Big Mouth? Are you known as the church rebel or the peacemaker? Is your reputation holy and upright or troublesome and devilish?

Look at verse 3 of this same chapter. Korah and his fleshly clan actually told Moses he went too far this time. They claimed that he had set himself up above the Lord's assembly. Wow! Don't we hear things like this often today: "Who made you the boss, preacher?" "What makes your decisions so right?" "Why should you have the final say?" "Why won't you submit to us?" "We outnumber you, and we are all holy."

Notice here that these words did not line up with their lifestyle. This is always a good Bible way to discern if someone has a Korah-like spirit. These 250 men said, "We are the appointed ones. We are members of the board. We are all holy." Listen, friend, any baby knows that you can't give speeches like this while you are in the midst of an insolent takeover/uprisal.

Just like in our churches today, Korah and these men wanted Moses OUT! They wanted him out so they could be the authority and have the final word on all matters. Do you know what is the funny part of this? Korah motivated these men to do this evil work, and then after it was done, he would have announced that he was going to be the new Moses. This is the way it always works. One man stirs up others against what they call a one-man show, and after they get rid of the one man, the originator makes his sly announcement that it isn't going to be a team effort any-more. I feel so very sorry for these poor defiled and deceived people.

Verses 8 and 9 may help us understand some of the drive these people have. Moses challenged them and reminded them that they had been hand-selected by God to the ministry of helps and should be very satisfied to be lay workers. In verse 10 Moses says, ". . . but now you are trying to get the priesthood too." The truth is, these people were not qualified for this. These people were not qualified for the priesthood, and even if they were, God didn't assign them to it. Besides, these rebellious, mouthy, and contemptuous people really thought they were quarreling with or attacking Moses. This fallacy is blasted to pieces in verse 11: "It is against the LORD that you and all your followers have banded together." Nauseating, isn't it? People who know to do good and know Bible principles lay their spirituality aside and go 100 percent flesh, thinking they are warring against men and find out (when it's too late) that they are accountable to God. Listen to me! When you mess with God's man, you're messing with God. Read Acts 9:1-5, and see what Jesus Himself told Paul about treating the Church and its leaders badly.

Back to Numbers, chapter 16. I don't think you ever want to be a person similar to those found in verse 12. I have had people leave the church I pastor—some to go home, some to start new works, some to live in sin, and some to follow a Korah spirit. It always concerns me that they slip away slyly, sneaking and crawling like snakes. I wonder why these people can't be mature enough to explain to church leaders why they are leaving and then keep their smutty mouths shut after they leave. Of course, if they were this mature, they probably wouldn't be leaving.

God does call some (very few) people out of the local church. You can read and see how this is done in Acts, chapter 13. The other ways of leaving are fleshly and devilish.

There are people all over the world who have a satanic, fleshly vendetta against pastors and other ministers. What a shame! What a ministry, huh?—to go around town defaming and vomiting on everyone the trash you feel you must minister to them. Be a minister of light, love, and Christ, not a vicious whirlwind of strife and malice.

I have had different sheep and some goats slip from the flock. When I call for them, they do one of two things. If they are humble, holy, clean sheep, they come running back to their fold. If they have a spirit like Korah, they say, "We will not come!" just like verse 12 says. They yell out all of their bowels. They scream things like, "And now you also want to lord it over us." "You are a cult leader, and this is a cult." "Don't you use these cult tactics on me!" "You are wrong, and I am right." "Does the Lord speak only through the pastor [Moses]?" And much more childish, carnal sewage.

> *"Just as Jannes and Jambres opposed Moses, so also these men oppose the truth—men of depraved minds, who, as far as the faith is concerned, are rejected.*
>
> *But they will not get very far because, as in the case of those men, their folly will be clear to everyone."*
>
> 2 Timothy 3:8-9 (NIV)

> *". . . Lovers of themselves, lovers of money, boastful, proud, abusive, disobedient to their parents, ungrateful, unholy,*
>
> *without love, unforgiving, slanderous, without self-control, brutal, not lovers of the good,*
>
> *treacherous, rash, conceited, lovers of pleasure rather than lovers of God . . ."*
>
> 2 Timothy 3:2-4 (NIV)

The Korah Spirit
Summary

1. You will not like your pastor's style of leadership.

2. You will think the congregation is holy and the preacher is shaky.

3. You will have problems, suspecting the preacher is stealing the money.

4. You will want to be a board member or in another leadership position so you can change what you don't like.

5. You will watch and judge the preacher rather than obey the Word and help the people.

6. You will band people together against the pastor in home meetings, or you will start a petition of impeachment.

7. You will begin to openly challenge your spiritual leaders.

8. You will think the anointing has left, and you will yell "cult," "unfair," etc.

9. You will ultimately leave the church yourself because your scheme failed, and your pride will drive you out.

The Korah Spirit
Quiz

Ask yourself these questions:

1. Do I have a hard time with my pastor having authority?

2. Do I feel he is unfair with the demand he puts on me to perform in spiritual things?

3. Do I often want to band with someone else and speak wrong against my pastor?

4. Do I feel that "250 plus me" is more secure leadership than just one man?

5. Am I often dissatisfied with the ministry of helps, and do I go on a campaign to get into the priesthood?

6. Am I often challenging that my pastor is being too hard or abrasive in his dealings with the flock?

7. Do I yell "cult," "unfair," "too strong," "too much control" about my pastor?

8. Do I quite often find the need to go tell others what I feel and see just to get it off my chest, even if it is gossip or murmuring?

If you answered yes to any of these questions, you are in trouble with God. Fast, pray, and go for mature spiritual help from a reputable minister of the gospel of Christ. If you have spoken to others, you should go and mend it. You have sinned, and you are accountable to God for it.

CHAPTER 3
THE SPIRIT OF JEZEBEL

"The Spirit of Hatred and Seduction"

The Jezebel spirit is one that leads you to hatred. You will turn from your love walk and begin to devour and seduce the holy leaders of the Lord.

You ladies, especially, watch out!

Text: 1 Kings 18, 19, and 21

Before we look into these scriptures, let me remind you that we are not doing a study on certain Bible characters but on the spirits that led and hindered them. Today many people read these Bible stories and wonder how anyone could be like Korah, Absalom, or Jezebel, while they themselves may be obtaining some of these exact problems. With this in mind, let's read on.

> *"For it was so, when Jezebel cut off the prophets of the LORD, that Obadiah took an hundred prophets, and hid them by fifty in a cave, and fed them with bread and water . . ."*
>
> 1 Kings 18:4

> *"Was it not told my lord what I did when Jezebel slew the prophets of the LORD, how I hid an hundred men*

*of the LORD'S prophets by fifty in a cave, and fed them
with bread and water?"*

1 Kings 18:13

*"And Ahab told Jezebel all that Elijah had done, and
withal how he had slain all the prophets with the
sword.*

*Then Jezebel sent a messenger unto Elijah, saying, So
let the gods do to me, and more also, if I make not thy
life as the life of one of them by to morrow about this
time."*

1 Kings 19:1-2

Jezebel was a woman, the wife of Ahab (one of the
most evil kings ever to reign). They truly deserved each
other and made a good pair. (Actually they were a very *bad*
pair.)

Jezebel actually had no authority of her own. She was
simply the wife of one who had authority. However, she
consistently borrowed, stole, and misused the king's throne
and his power.

The spirit of this woman drove her to get what she
wanted no matter what the cost. She couldn't stand anyone
to deny her or her husband. She was very power-thirsty and
wicked.

Jezebel hated the prophets of God because they served
differently than her. They prophesied to the people what
God said, so she was threatened by them. Jezzy was a very
nervous, shifty woman. She wanted people to serve Baal,
not Jehovah. As you well know, God's men don't go for
this—not even if the government decrees it. Finally the
lady seduced her husband and other prophets and even
began to slay the true prophets of the Lord. Jezebel could

not stand to think that someone had more favor than her.

One day her husband asked a palace neighbor to sell him his well-kept vineyard. After all, it was real close to the palace walls, and hubby wanted it. Hey, with this spirit, whatever hubby wants, he can have as long as it doesn't cost *her* anything. Jezzy went and put a letter out on Naboth, the vineyard owner. Then two spies were dispatched to smut his name and bring lies against him. The end result: Naboth was dragged out of town and stoned. Jezzy got the vineyard for hubby, and they went down to possess it. All was going just fine for the evil crew, until Elijah and God . . . God directed Elijah to meet them at the vineyard. Elijah met them, and this is the outcome.

> ". . . *Thus saith the LORD, Hast thou killed, and also taken possession? And thou shalt speak unto him, saying, Thus saith the LORD, In the place where dogs licked the blood of Naboth shall dogs lick thy blood, even thine.*
>
> *And Ahab said to Elijah, Hast thou found me, O mine enemy? And he answered, I have found thee: because thou hast sold thyself to work evil in the sight of the LORD.*
>
> *And of Jezebel also spake the LORD, saying, The dogs shall eat Jezebel by the wall of Jezreel."*
>
> 1 Kings 21:19-20, 23

If you wish, you can study verses 25-29 and also chapter 22, verses 36-40, to see the poor end result.

Hey, Sister, if I were you, I wouldn't commune with this spirit in my heart and mind, let alone even get near it.

Jezebel died along with Ahab, but what do you suppose happened to that driving spirit that kept her in the flesh, hating everyone and seeking the chief seats? You're right. It's roaming around today wanting to rest on you and make friends with you. I hope you aren't that desperate for friends!

Today in the church world, this spirit works desperately hard to get on women. Satan wants to drive these women to rule over whatever authority their husband has.

I've seen this Jezzy spirit begin to minister to women, and they slowly walk out of line, get out of order, and begin to hate and speak filthy things against the prophets or pastor. These women push for control—in the home, marriage, church, pulpit, work—everywhere. They must be in charge, and they will kill the pastor's reputation in order to influence others. They constantly mutilate the pastor's reputation as they put themselves up for positions and leadership availability.

It's like the woman who said, "There are no good pastors and no good churches to go to, so I'm going to just stay home." When asked by a friend how things were going, she responded with, "Things are great, never been better. In fact, we have started a Bible study in our home for all of those people who have been hurt by that mean preacher. Want to join us?" "Who is speaking there?" the friend asked. "Oh, I am," said the lady who goes to church nowhere, has no pastor, and bears forth no noticeable fruit.

You know, the saddest part of that story is this: There really are Christians who are so naive and ignorant that they will actually go and fellowship with and listen to someone this unfruitful. What a waste! What a shame! How foolish!

Jezebel-spirited people want the pastor or minister dead, driven out of town, or totally stripped of his power. Don't be part of it. I don't want to do your funeral, and we don't want dogs to lap up your blood—or your son's!

Check out this scripture passage.

"'As for you, my flock, this is what the Sovereign LORD says: I will judge between one sheep and another, and between rams and goats.

Is it not enough for you to feed on the good pasture? Must you also trample the rest of your pasture with your feet? Is it not enough for you to drink clear water? Must you also muddy the rest with your feet?"

Ezekiel 34:17-18 (NIV)

This is exactly what demons want to use you to do. Eat what you enjoy, and ruin all the rest for everybody else. Drink what is good for you, but speak bad about what you don't like so no one else can enjoy it either. This is exactly what they want you to do.

The Jezebel Spirit
Summary

1. It mostly ministers to women.

2. You will desire the "upper hand."

3. You will want to have the final and upmost voice.

4. You will begin to connive and cheat to get ahead.

5. You will begin to hate the brisk-walking, straight-talking preaching.

6. You will be jealous of the prophets and their popularity, gifts, and anointings.

7. You will turn to be totally self-centered and follow after your own desires.

8. You will constantly speak against and wrestle with God's leaders.

9. Your marriage will be miserable.

The Jezebel Spirit
Quiz

Ladies, ask yourselves these questions:

1. Do I often want to shut the preacher's mouth?

2. Do I wrestle with gifts and prophesies that I don't deliver?

3. Do I always try to domineer and overpower my husband, boss, pastor, and friends?

4. Do I often turn from love to hate or from support to opposition in my relationship with my pastor?

5. Do I get hurt, bitter, or mad because I personally can't be close, intimate friends with my pastor?

6. Do I get easily offended when I am corrected and because of that strike out against the leadership?

7. Do I see myself out to gain things, money, prestige, position, or popularity?

If you answered yes to any of these questions, you are in trouble with God. Fast, pray, and go for mature spiritual help from a reputable minister of the gospel of Christ.

CHAPTER 4
THE SPIRIT OF ABSALOM

"The Jealous Spirit of Conspiracy"

The Absalom spirit is one that will lead you into realms of jealousy. You will be jealous of other believers, ministers, and even family members. This spirit will cause you to be part of a conspiracy against your spiritual leaders.

Text: 2 Samuel 15 and 18

> *"And it came to pass after this, that Absalom prepared him chariots and horses, and fifty men to run before him.*
>
> *And Absalom rose up early, and stood beside the way of the gate: and it was so, that when any man that had a controversy came to the king for judgment, then Absalom called unto him, and said, Of what city art thou? And he said, Thy servant is of one of the tribes of Israel.*
>
> *And Absalom said unto him, See, thy matters are good and right; but there is no man deputed of the king to hear thee.*
>
> *Absalom said moreover, Oh that I were made judge in the land, that every man which hath any suit or cause might come unto me, and I would do him justice!*

And it was so, that when any man came nigh to him to do him obeisance, he put forth his hand, and took him, and kissed him.

And on this manner did Absalom to all Israel that came to the king for judgment: so Absalom stole the hearts of the men of Israel."

2 Samuel 15:1-6

This is pretty low. This is bad, folks, when a man will do things this bad behind his own father's back just to make himself look good. What a little rebel he was. Absalom would degrade his own dad's reputation by complaining about his ability to judge and run the kingdom. Absalom was even found embracing and kissing cheeks of men he wanted to gain favor with. This is the ultimate of political maneuver—kissing of cheeks!

Absalom actually worked on these people behind the king's back until he stole their hearts. They began to believe Absalom and doubt David. They thought Absalom was sweet and caring and that David was bold and hard.

I'll tell you, friend, many, many people do this same exact thing in the church today. This is especially true among assistant leaders. They get jealous of the number one man, so they politick the people toward them and against their pastor. They get jealous of the ministry that pastor has, and they try to have one just as good without paying the price. It won't work! But this is what the Absalom spirit will drive you to do.

"If I were the king . . ." This is a very famous saying. "If I were the pastor . . ." This one is just as famous. I hear it all the time as I travel across our nation. For some reason young ministers are really prey to this as well as deacons

25

and elders in local churches. If these people ever did obtain the pastorate, it would be disastrous. Anyone who would politick this way for position would mutilate himself in office. These people are so deceived.

Absalom actually coerced and gathered men together to march against the throne. He was real proud of the army he gathered. He really thought they would amount to something.

Did you notice what Absalom told the people who came to the king for help and counseling? He told them that they each had legitimate claims but that there was no one from the king's office to help. I hear this all the time. It's so easy to say the pastor is too busy; he just doesn't have time for us; he hasn't set anyone in the right office to help us; I guess we are on our own. How sad and how sickening it is that people thrive on such self-pity. Actually they are obtaining an Absalom-like spirit.

Well, Absalom finally did it. He collected enough radicals to march against the king. He really thought he could win. (How stupid.) That day there was a great war, and many men died. David won—of course. Absalom ended in a sad way, yet it's almost a joke. Read this:

> "Now Absalom happened to meet David's men. He was riding his mule, and as the mule went under the thick branches of a large oak, Absalom's head got caught in the tree. He was left hanging in midair, while the mule he was riding kept on going.
>
> Joab said, 'I'm not going to wait like this for you.' So he took three javelins in his hand and plunged them into Absalom's heart while Absalom was still alive in the oak tree."

> 2 Samuel 18:9, 14 (NIV)

Today in our churches there are Absaloms who think they can kiss cheeks and shake hands with everyone to gain favor. They talk about the pastor and his inefficiency in office. They dream about themselves becoming pastors. It's the same spirit that was on Absalom. One day, after they gather enough ill-reputed men and women on their side, they will try to overthrow the pulpit, even at the cost of splitting the church. You know, men like this really don't care too much for anyone or anything but themselves. They are too power-hungry, too prestige-thirsty. It's sad to say, but they will be left hanging someday realizing that they have reaped what they have sown.

Don't let it be you. Stay away from these kinds of criminal bands. Watch out for Absalom.

Oh yes, one more thing: Watch out for the pastor's number one chief warrior, because he's waiting for the day you hang yourself. You might just find that his love and dedication to the pastor is stronger than your jealousy and conspiracy.

The Absalom Spirit
Summary

1. You will begin to judge your own family members.

2. You will begin to wish you were in charge.

3. You will think and say, "If I were the pastor . . ."

4. You will be convinced that your pastor is too busy for you and that no one else could even help you.

5. You will feel comfortable running with those who have been placed under church discipline and those who are troublemakers. You will have carnal sympathy for them.

6. You will start to collect people who share the same problems you have.

7. You will begin to politick, kiss cheeks, and put down your pastor.

8. You will accuse your pastor of being too hard, strict, and untouchable.

9. You will finally march against your church leadership but only to your own failure.

The Absalom Spirit
Quiz

Ask yourself these questions:

1. Do I feel my pastor is too hard or too strict?

2. Do I often find the need to go and share things that bother me with other people?

3. Do I try to band together with people who have the same problems I do?

4. Am I politicking, kissing cheeks, or licking the wounds of people who have hurt feelings and charges against church leadership?

5. Do I ever think or say, "If I were the pastor . . ."?

6. Do I find myself most comfortable when I am with troubled people rather than pure and holy fruit-bearers?

If you answered yes to any of these questions, you are in trouble with God. Fast, pray, and go for mature spiritual help from a reputable minister of the gospel of Christ.

CHAPTER 5
THE SAULISH SPIRIT

"The Religious and Prideful Spirit"

The Saulish spirit is one that leads you into self-centeredness and pride. You will end up in religion, and you will deny the power of true Christianity.

Text: 1 Samuel 9 and 28

> ". . . Saul, a choice young man, and a goodly: and there was not among the children of Israel a goodlier person than he: from his shoulders and upward he was higher than any of the people."
>
> 1 Samuel 9:2

> "And when Samuel saw Saul, the LORD said unto him, Behold the man whom I spake to thee of! this same shall reign over my people."
>
> 1 Samuel 9:17

I purposely started with these scriptures because I wanted you to see that most bad, spoiled, and troubled Christians all start out good, just like Saul. He started out so good. He was a good person, and God appointed him to be a ruler over His people. The Prophet Samuel was also impressed by him, so it started out well for Saul. This is the way it is for most people today. They start out fine. Their attitude is good, and they serve the Lord well. Somehow, through the months or years, they begin to grow weary or get hurt or disappointed, and then, just like Saul, they begin to say and do bad things.

Saul somehow obtained a religious spirit which slowly led him away from the true presence of God. He began to challenge the priests and even offer his own sacrifices. He slowly came to the decision that he didn't need any priests at all in his life. In fact, he grew so hardhearted and bitter that he refused to let the prophet minister to the soldiers before entering battle. One day he even referred to himself as the sacrifice for God.

There are people just like this today. They follow these exact steps. First they change from Holy Spirit leadership to religious-spirit leadership. Then they begin to grow bitter and hardhearted. Soon they are pushing the pastor out of the way and doing their own ministry. It won't be long until their self-centeredness and pride will lift them so high they will be worthless to God.

> *"Samuel also said unto Saul, The LORD sent me to anoint thee to be king over his people, over Israel: now therefore hearken thou unto the voice of the words of the LORD."*

1 Samuel 15:1

> *"Now go and smite Amalek, and utterly destroy all that they have, and spare them not; but slay both man and woman, infant and suckling, ox and sheep, camel and ass."*

1 Samuel 15:3

> *"And Saul smote the Amalekites from Havilah until thou comest to Shur, that is over against Egypt.*

31

*And he took Agag the king of the Amalekites alive,
and utterly destroyed all the people with the edge of
the sword.*

*But Saul and the people spared Agag, and the best of
the sheep, and of the oxen, and of the fatlings, and the
lambs, and all that was good, and would not utterly
destroy them. . . ."*

1 Samuel 15:7-9

Oh no! God's man just fell, and the people were in
agreement with it. God said to utterly destroy all. Everything and every one of the enemies were to be utterly
destroyed, but the Bible says that Saul and the people
would not do it.

There are so many people like this today. They know
what God said, but they still will not do it. The penalty for
such treason and mutiny is very severe.

It's so easy to obey God. I don't know why so many
people outwardly disobey him. I guess their pride and self-
centeredness steal their fear of God.

One of the ramifications of sin that most people don't
enjoy is the prophet's confrontation. Samuel came right
away and rebuked the king. But Saul cried out how he had
served the Lord so well and done all that God had com-
manded. The prophet actually had to bring his attention to
it!

Read verses 10-19 of this chapter in the Bible. They
will show you how people—even leaders—squirm under
the prophet's ministry.

I watch this happen quite often. People know what to
do to be obedient to Christ, but somehow they just don't

obey. Then when they do sin, they don't see it. They accuse the prophet of being prejudiced or touchy. My friend, you are in deep trouble when you sin and don't even realize it. You are in bigger trouble when a spiritual leader points it out to you, and you still make excuses for it or even deny you did it or said it.

Look at the verses below, and see what Saul had to say about his sin.

> *"And Saul said unto Samuel, Yea, I have obeyed the voice of the LORD, and have gone the way which the LORD sent me, and have brought Agag the king of Amalek, and have utterly destroyed the Amalekites.*
>
> *But the people took of the spoil, sheep and oxen, the chief of the things which should have been utterly destroyed, to sacrifice unto the LORD thy God in Gilgal."*
>
> 1 Samuel 15:20-21

Isn't that something? Saul actually blamed his disobedience and poor leadership on the people. He said, "It's the people's fault. They did this." Notice also that both Saul and the people disobeyed the Lord, and then rather than confessing it, they excused their sin by saying they did it with God in mind. "We only wanted to keep the pure things that would be beneficial in our walk with God." How sad. These people didn't realize that God knew best. God knew what was good and bad.

There are plenty of people like this today. They get prideful and real religious about things, and then they step out of line or out of order. When correction comes, they always have some "religious" excuse for their sin and disobedience. Many times they are just like Saul, and they blame other people for their actions.

This next verse will prove to you that Saul had a real pride problem.

"And Samuel said, When thou wast little in thine own sight, wast thou not made the head of the tribes of Israel, and the LORD anointed thee king over Israel?"

1 Samuel 15:17

You see, many leaders are like Saul. In fact, many people who are not leaders have this very problem. They are real sweet and humble before the Lord. The Lord lifts them up and begins to use them. They do well and begin to advance in the kingdom of God. Soon, they get lifted up in themselves and begin to make decisions on their own. They get too big for their britches, and then they disobey God.

Remember this: Religion clouds your convictions, and it dilutes your power in Christ. Pride always justifies your feelings and actions, and it always lifts self up above everything and everyone else.

Do you know that some people are so deeply in trouble spiritually that they turn against the priests (pastors)? That's right! That's one of the strongholds this Saulish spirit has on people. It tells people that they don't need the spiritual leader and that they don't need any help. "I will do this myself." "I will make my own sacrifices." "I will kill the priest or his reputation if I have to just to get ahold of what I want." "Who needs this pastor, anyway?" "He's too hard." "He's too strict for me." "He's always dealing with negative things." "He's always talking about me in his sermons."

Hey, there is more, much more. These are just a few of the things that Saulish people say.

Check out these scriptures:

1 Samuel 15:23-24
Saul failed as leader; he feared the people.

1 Samuel 18:8-9
Jealousy consumed his heart.

1 Samuel 20:33
Saul threw javelins and wanted to kill.

1 Samuel 22:19
Saul killed priests because they wouldn't join up with him.

1 Samuel 16:14, 18:10
Saul eventually was possessed by an evil spirit of religion.

2 Samuel 6:14-16
His daughter despised worship to the Lord.

1 Samuel 15:27-28
Saul lashed out at the prophet.

1 Samuel 13:9-12
Saul played priest for a day.

1 Samuel 28:1-9
Saul sought help from a witch.

1 Samuel 31:4-6
Saul committed suicide.

> *"And as Samuel turned about to go away, he laid hold upon the skirt of his mantle, and it rent.*
>
> *And Samuel said unto him, The LORD hath rent the kingdom of Israel from thee this day, and hath given it to a neighbour of thine, that is better than thou."*
>
> 1 Samuel 15:27-28

This is so typical. Saul lashed out at the prophet. He

actually rent his priestly, or prophetic, garments. You know what happened to Saul from there.

Listen, friends, so many people today are just like Saul. They start out so good and so humble. They seem to do so well for some time, and then it's a downhill decline. They start out in jealousy, then religious activity, then putting down the priests, then offering their own sacrifice, then throwing javelins, then framing their own loved ones, then rampaging the kingdom like a tyrant out of control, and so on.

I hope you don't end up like Saul. It's terrible to die as one who had never been anointed. Even worse is when you die with no anointing because you did yourself in. (Read 2 Sam. 1:21.)

This Saulish spirit wants to fellowship with you and have a conversation with you. This demon wants to talk to your head. You guard yourself biblically. Quit meditating in negatives, and please don't be a trash collector.

When religion (diluted, counterfeit Christianity) comes your way, throw it out. Don't be your own priest. When jealousy and pride rise up within you, cast them down—tell them to get lost!

I pray to God you will stay humble and obey Him.

It would be good for you not to have a priest's blood on your hands or in your record. Don't rent any mantles today!

The Saulish Spirit
Summary

1. Always works on God's chosen ones and their family members.

2. It will cause you to turn on your own helpers.

3. You will begin to be jealous of others' accomplishments.

4. You will begin to disobey God and not realize it.

5. You will lash out toward the prophets when correction comes to you.

6. You will play priest and begin to handle your own sacraments.

7. You will harm God's mantle and His priests.

8. You will lose your humility and become arrogant and right in your own eyes.

9. You will fear the people.

The Saulish Spirit
Quiz

Ask yourself these questions:

1. Do I get jealous of other believers or ministries?

2. Do I lash out at my leaders when I am corrected?

3. Do I always have to be confronted with my sin because I don't see it in time?

4. Do I make excuses for my sinful words and actions?

5. Do I often feel I could make it okay without any spiritual leadership?

6. Do I sometimes despise outbursts of worship like shouts, dancing, etc.?

7. Do I often think more highly of myself than I ought?

If you answered yes to any of these questions, you are in trouble with God. Fast, pray, and go for mature spiritual help from a reputable minister of the gospel of Christ.

CHAPTER 6
THE ISCARIOT SPIRIT

"The Spirit of Sneaky Betrayal and Confused Repentance"

BEWARE ... This spirit will influence you to sell out your leader and die in suicide.

"Then one of the twelve, called Judas Iscariot, went unto the chief priests,

And said unto them, What will ye give me, and I will deliver him unto you? And they covenanted with him for thirty pieces of silver.

And from that time he sought opportunity to betray him."

Matthew 26:14-16

Remember that we are talking about the spirit that drove Iscariot to do what he did. The man Judas died, but the spirit that influenced him is still on the earth. As I expose this demon in this chapter, you will have to admit that it is still ministering to church people today.

Judas was chosen to be one of the twelve but never really seemed to be of the same spirit and heart of the others.

39

He was often questioning some of the things that Jesus did. He seemed to present a spiritual attitude that was higher than the others' and sometimes even higher than Jesus'.

> *"Then Jesus six days before the passover came to Bethany, where Lazarus was which had been dead, whom he raised from the dead.*
>
> *There they made him a supper; and Martha served: but Lazarus was one of them that sat at the table with him.*
>
> *Then took Mary a pound of ointment of spikenard, very costly, and anointed the feet of Jesus, and wiped his feet with her hair: and the house was filled with the odour of the ointment.*
>
> *Then saith one of his disciples, Judas Iscariot, Simon's son, which should betray him,*
>
> *Why was not this ointment sold for three hundred pence, and given to the poor?"*

John 12:1-5

Isn't it something that Judas displays that superficial spirituality here and voices his great care for the poor. This spirit always causes people to be concerned about how the preacher uses the money and displays an extra concern for the people.

He just couldn't stand the fact that someone was giving the preacher attention instead of giving it to him. He wasn't concerned for the poor. This was an indictment against the character and integrity of Jesus.

When this demon begins to indoctrinate people, they will become more and more suspicious of the preachers.

Eventually they will openly challenge the preachers' integrity.

> *"But, behold, the hand of him that betrayeth me is with me on the table.*
>
> *And truly the Son of man goeth, as it was determined: but woe unto that man by whom he is betrayed!*
>
> *And they began to enquire among themselves, which of them it was that should do this thing."*
>
> Luke 22:21-23

Pay very close attention here as I reveal to you one of the most deadly things about this demon. This spirit made Judas an undetectable imitator and pretender.

The other eleven never suspected Judas as a traitor. In fact when Jesus told the twelve that there was a betrayer among them, they couldn't figure out who it was.

This spirit will cause you to pretend to be a real Christian so well that only you will know the difference. We see this every day in the churches of the '90s.

> *"When Jesus had thus said, he was troubled in spirit, and testified, and said, Verily, verily, I say unto you, that one of you shall betray me.*
>
> *Then **the disciples looked one on another, doubting of whom he spake**.*
>
> *Now there was leaning on Jesus' bosom one of his disciples, whom Jesus loved.*
>
> *Simon Peter therefore beckoned to him, that he should ask who it should be of whom he spake.*
>
> *He then lying on Jesus' breast saith unto him, Lord, who is it?*

> *Jesus answered, He it is, to whom I shall give a sop,*
> *when I have dipped it. And when he had dipped the*
> *sop, he gave it to Judas Iscariot, the son of Simon.*
>
> *And after the sop Satan entered into him. Then said*
> *Jesus unto him, That thou doest, do quickly.*
>
> *Now no man at the table knew for what intent he*
> *spake this unto him.*
>
> **For some of them thought, because Judas had the**
> **bag,** *that Jesus had said unto him, Buy those things*
> *that we have need of against the feast; or, that he*
> *should give something to the poor.*
>
> **He then having received the sop went immediately**
> **out***: and it was night."*

John 13:21-30

Once again it is easy to see that when Jesus labeled Judas, the twelve still didn't really catch on. This is a sign of just how convincing Judas's pretense was. Even after Jesus marked him in the face of them all, they were still sort of disillusioned.

This spirit will not only take control of the vessel that yields to it, but it will also confuse and disillusion those around it. It will make it real difficult for a leader to ever expose the betrayer because the others may want to side with or go with him.

I want you to see that all the time Judas was with Jesus and under that anointing he seemed to fit right in, but as soon as he was in another environment, he fit in there.

This spirit will cause you to have a dual personality and a dual vocabulary—one when you are around the other Christians and another when you are with the world or the religious crowd. Your values will get all misconstrued, and you will make all the wrong choices, causing you to abandon "right" and partner "wrong." Many people who are ministered to by this demon literally ruin their lives and never recover. In Judas's case he ended up in suicide.

> *"Then Judas, which had betrayed him, when he saw that he was condemned,* ***repented*** *himself, and brought again the thirty pieces of silver to the chief priests and elders,*
>
> ***Saying, I have sinned*** *in that I have betrayed the innocent blood. And they said, What is that to us? see thou to that.*
>
> *And he cast down the pieces of silver in the temple, and departed,* ***and went and hanged himself."***
>
> Matthew 27:3-5

Notice in the scripture just quoted that Judas repented but to the wrong people. He repented to the people he sinned with rather than the people he sinned against. I see many people practice this deceiving form of repentance and really end up no better off than Judas.

In fact suicide has actually been predicted to be one of the top killers of the end-time people. I wonder in many cases if it isn't this same spirit. You see, feeling bad about your sin isn't enough. You must have godly sorrow if you are going to really turn from it and find true repentance. You must not only admit you sinned but go to the people whom you sinned against.

The people Judas sinned with were not really the friends they made on to be. They used him to the max, and he didn't even realize it.

Judas was also very sneaky. This spirit that influenced him made him kind of slimy in the ways he sneaked around Jesus and mocked the covenant behind His back. In fact he literally sold his pastor to the killer crowd for money. Do you think there was a connection between this kind of betrayal and the fact that Judas carried the money bag for Jesus' whole ministry?

> *"But Jesus said unto him, **Judas, betrayest thou the Son of man with a kiss?"***
>
> Luke 22:48

> *"And Judas also, which betrayed him, knew the place: for Jesus ofttimes resorted thither with his disciples."*
>
> John 18:2

All the time Judas was selling Jesus he was still going to all the meetings. In fact Judas stayed to the very "last" supper before Jesus finally marked him.

Notice that the betrayer actually pointed out Jesus with a kiss. This is as low as you can get. Right in front of the other disciples Judas kisses Jesus so the enemy can take Him. This demon will get stronger and stronger on you if you fellowship with it at all. It will cause you to get bolder about your covert activities.

Notice also that Judas knew right where Jesus and His key men would be. When he was under that sweet anointing of Jesus, he himself at times felt the rush of the Spirit of God in his soul. Here he used this memory of past intimacy as a weapon of high treason.

Bind this spirit and cast down every thought pertaining to it. Be strong and godly when you are around those who have already succumbed to its influence.

The Iscariot Spirit
Summary

1. This spirit will slowly cause you to have a dual personality, one when with Christians and one when not.

2. It will make you a perfect pretender.

3. It will cause you to betray your leaders with a kiss.

4. It will cause you to question even the integrity of Christ and His Word.

5. You will be responsible for the people around you whom you deceive.

6. This spirit will cause you to be sneaky.

7. You will eventually trade your walk with Christ for money.

8. You will want to repent but to the people you sinned with instead of the ones you sinned against.

9. This demon fellowships very closely with the spirit of suicide.

The Iscariot Spirit
Quiz

Ask yourself these questions:

1. Do you ever wonder why the other disciples always seem to be more committed than you?

2. Do you find yourself acting less Christian when you are around unsaved people?

3. Does money seem to be real important to you?

4. Are you jealous of your pastor and concerned about the amount of attention that he gets?

5. Do you allow people to talk against your church and pastor in front of you, and do you say nothing in their defense?

6. Does anyone in your life really know what you are like in private, and do you try to avoid them because of what they know?

7. Do you repent to people you sin with instead of the ones you sin against?

8. Do you ever fight the thoughts of suicide?

If you answered yes to any of the above questions, you are in trouble with God. Fast, pray, and go for mature spiritual help from a reputable minister of the gospel of Christ.

CHAPTER 7
THE SPIRIT OF THE TEN SPIES

"The Contagious Spirit of
Unbelief and Quitting"

BEWARE . . . This spirit will cause you to doubt God, resist your leader, and turn back to Egypt.

"Behold, the LORD thy God hath set the land before thee: go up and possess it, as the LORD God of thy fathers hath said unto thee; fear not, neither be discouraged.

And ye came near unto me every one of you, and said, We will send men before us, and they shall search us out the land, and bring us word again by what way we must go up, and into what cities we shall come.

And the saying pleased me well: and I took twelve men of you, one of a tribe:

And they turned and went up into the mountain, and came unto the valley of Eshcol, and searched it out.

And they took of the fruit of the land in their hands, and brought it down unto us, and brought us word again, and said, It is a good land which the LORD our God doth give us.

Notwithstanding ***ye would not go up, but rebelled
against the commandment of the Lord*** *your God:*

And ***ye murmured in your tents,*** *and said, Because
the Lord hated us, he hath brought us forth out of the
land of Egypt, to deliver us into the hand of the
Amorites, to destroy us."*

Deuteronomy 1:21-27

The spirit of these ten spies is one that will cause you
to die on the wrong side of the river—the wrong side of the
promises of God.

These ten spies stirred up the whole congregation to the
degree that those walking in faith could not change the
people's minds. Caleb, Joshua, and Moses couldn't even
calm the crowd.

One of the major contentions of this demon is that it
causes people to quit and expect God to do it all. Don't
even try to tell me that this spirit isn't whispering to people
today—yes, even church people—in fact maybe mostly
church people.

You see these ten spies were disturbed that they had
wandered for 40 years, and now they have found the
promise land just to discover that God wasn't just turning it
over to them. They thought that they had done enough to
inherit the promises. They were put out that God wasn't
just going to hand it to them.

They recognized that it was the land God promised, but
they were afraid of the giants and the fortified cities.
Joshua and Caleb took it as a righteous challenge and
wanted to go possess it.

When you let this demon minister to you, you become

weak in faith and expect God to do it all. "If God want is me to have it, He will just come right down here and give it to me." Wrong!

This spirit causes you to have a very small and twisted view and opinion of yourself. These men said that their enemies saw them the same way they saw themselves—as grasshoppers. Listen to yourself. Do you have grasshopper reports that stir up the people, or do you have a faith report that cuts down the enemy? It could be the very thing that causes you to die on the wrong side of the river without the promises of God.

> *"And they returned from searching of the land after forty days.*
>
> *And they went and came to Moses, and to Aaron, and to all the congregation of the children of Israel, unto the wilderness of Paran, to Kadesh; and brought back word unto them, and unto all the congregation, and shewed them the fruit of the land.*
>
> *And they told him, and said, We came unto the land whither thou sentest us, and surely it floweth with milk and honey; and this is the fruit of it.*
>
> *Nevertheless the people be strong that dwell in the land, and the cities are walled, and very great: and moreover we saw the children of Anak there.*
>
> *The Amalekites dwell in the land of the south: and the Hittites, and the Jebusites, and the Amorites, dwell in the mountains: and the Canaanites dwell by the sea, and by the coast of Jordan.*
>
> *And Caleb stilled the people before Moses, and said, Let us go up at once, and possess it; for we are well able to overcome it.*
>
> *But the men that went up with him said, We be not*

able to go up against the people; for they are stronger than we.

*And **they brought up an evil report** of the land which they had searched unto the children of Israel, saying, The land, through which we have gone to search it, is a land that eateth up the inhabitants thereof; and all the people that we saw in it are men of a great stature.*

And there we saw the giants, the sons of Anak, which come of the giants: and we were in our own sight as grasshoppers, and so we were in their sight."

Numbers 13:25-33

*"And all the **congregation lifted up their voice, and cried; and the people wept that night.***

*And all the **children of Israel murmured against Moses** and against Aaron: and the whole congregation said unto them, Would God that we had died in the land of Egypt! or would God we had died in this wilderness!*

And wherefore hath the LORD brought us unto this land, to fall by the sword, that our wives and our children should be a prey? were it not better for us to return into Egypt?

And they said one to another, Let us make a captain, and let us return into Egypt."

Numbers 14:1-4

Beware of this anti-faith, anti-courage spirit and those who are influenced by it. If it gets on you, it will take you totally off course.

The Spirit of the Ten Spies
Summary

1. They were put out that God didn't just hand over their blessings.

2. They were so disappointed that "they" had to do something to obtain their blessings.

3. They saw themselves as grasshoppers.

4. This spirit will cause you to stir up the whole congregation.

5. This spirit will keep you in doubt and unbelief instead of faith.

6. This spirit will cause you to pay attention to your obstacles rather than the promises of God.

7. You will stay on the wrong side of the river and never really enjoy the blessings.

8. You will not only resist your leader in the Lord but actually rally against him.

The Spirit of the Ten Spies
Quiz

Ask yourself these questions:

1. Do you at times think that God should just hand over His goods to you without you doing anything?

2. Do you always look at the obstacles rather than God's ability to help you overcome them?

3. Do you ever stir up others in order to prove your point?

4. Do you ever rally against your leader in the Lord?

5. Who looks bigger to you–your giants or your God?

6. Do you see yourself as less than how the Word sees you?

7. Do you recognize the promises of God but feel you will never have them for yourself?

8. Do you feel your leader is not qualified to lead you into the promise land?

If you answered yes to any of these questions, you are in trouble with God. Fast, pray, and go for mature spiritual help from a reputable minister of the gospel of Christ.

CHAPTER 8
THE SPIRIT OF DEMAS

"The Spirit of the World"

BEWARE ... This spirit wants to use you to desert the preacher and go for the world.

*"Marcus, Aristarchus, **Demas**, Lucas, **my fellow-labourers**."*

Philemon 24

Demas was a fellow laborer of the Apostle Paul. It seems that he worked hand in hand with Paul and was part of the apostolic company that journeyed around the world preaching the gospel and building the Church.

The Apostle Paul by far had the most prominent ministry of the day, so Demas had a pretty high spot in the Church world as he worked with Paul.

"For Demas hath forsaken me, having loved this present world, and is departed unto Thessalonica; Crescens to Galatia, Titus unto Dalmatia."

2 Timothy 4:10

Paul described in the verses above that Demas was not with him anymore and in fact wasn't even in the ministry anymore. What is it besides a demonic influence that can cause a man to leave such a beautiful position in life and cash in his eternity?

I want you to see the three things that this spirit did in Demas's life. It does the same things today, and it is easy to see in some church members.

First, Demas forsook Paul. Forsaking your pastor and going with a stranger on your own is always the first sign of spiritual trouble of any kind.

Second, Demas fell in love (lust) with the world. Once you cast off restraint you are done. It's just a matter of time before you are of the world once again. When you grow cold and get your focus away from the visionary in your life, then you begin to be attracted to the worldly things. The Lord once said to me that the attractions of the world are really just distractions to the Christian.

Third, Demas departed. It is only a matter of time before you depart once you take the other two steps. Learn from Demas, and stay away from this spirit. Don't let it get on you, and don't fellowship with people who have it.

Demas died of course, but the demon satan assigned to his life to destroy him is still trying to duplicate its pattern on people today.

1. It coerces you to forsake your pastor.

2. It makes the things of this world not only look attractive but seem feasible to have and enjoy.

3. It causes you to become bold in denial and actually depart from the ministry God assigned you to.

Bind it in Jesus' name!

The Spirit of Demas
Summary

1. This spirit will cause you to look at the world and its things all the time you are walking with Christ.

2. The love for worldly things will draw you away from the church.

3. You will first forsake your preacher.

4. You will eventually depart from the ministry you are involved in and go for the world.

5. The seductive power of this spirit will actually lead you into the world that you once denounced.

The Spirit of Demas
Quiz

Ask yourself these questions:

1. Do you crave worldly things instead of the things of God?

2. Do you serve in the church but feel somewhat put out because of it?

3. Do you ever feel like God owes you something and that He should reward you for your service?

4. Does prosperity only mean money and possessions to you?

5. Do you feel the draw to pull away from the church and go for the goods?

6. Do you ever feel like your pastor is holding you back or postponing your promotion?

7. Do you at times feel like the best thing for you to do is depart and just go for the possessions and promotions in the world?

8. Do you ever get jealous when others get blessed?

If you answered yes to any of these questions, you are in trouble with God. Fast, pray, and go for mature spiritual help from a reputable minister of the gospel of Christ.

CHAPTER 9
THE SPIRIT OF GEHAZI

"The Spirit of Greed and Self-Seeking"

BEWARE . . . This spirit will make you self-seeking and sneaky. It will cause you to be leprous and even curse your children.

"But Gehazi, the servant of Elisha the man of God, said, Behold, my master hath spared Naaman this Syrian, in not receiving at his hands that which he brought: but, as the LORD liveth, I will run after him, and take somewhat of him.

So Gehazi followed after Naaman. And when Naaman saw him running after him, he lighted down from the chariot to meet him, and said, Is all well?

*And he said, All is well. **My master hath sent me**, saying, Behold, even now there be come to me from mount Ephraim two young men of the sons of the prophets: give them, I pray thee, a talent of silver, and two changes of garments.*

And Naaman said, Be content, take two talents. And he urged him, and bound two talents of silver in two bags, with two changes of garments, and laid them upon two of his servants; and they bare them before him.

*And when he came to the tower, he took them from their hand, and **bestowed them in the house**: and he let the men go, and they departed.*

*But he went in, and stood before his master. And Elisha said unto him, Whence comest thou, Gehazi? And he said, **Thy servant went no whither**.*

And he said unto him, Went not mine heart with thee, when the man turned again from his chariot to meet thee? Is it a time to receive money, and to receive garments, and oliveyards, and vineyards, and sheep, and oxen, and menservants, and maidservants?

*The **leprosy therefore of Naaman shall cleave unto thee, and unto thy seed for ever**. And he went out from his presence a leper as white as snow."*

2 Kings 5:20-27

This story has always amazed me. I could never figure out how on earth a man with this kind of favor and position could trade it all in for money.

Elisha turned down the general when he offered the prophet an offering for his services. The assistant, Gehazi, somehow couldn't understand this and decided he would reap the benefit. He chased down the general and lied to him. He told Naaman that Elisha had sent him and that he had changed his mind about the offering. This is a pretty severe lie. Lying about what your leader says and misquoting or misinterpreting him is part of the influence of this demon.

General Naaman paid a pretty sum, and his men delivered it to Gehazi's dwelling. Gehazi hid it there thinking somehow that the prophet would never know what he did. I wonder what Gehazi planned to spend it on. He was with the prophet every day. No matter how he spent it, Elisha would see the evidence.

I guess Gehazi lost track of the fact that his boss was a prophet. Elisha picked up his activities in the spirit realm and actually told Gehazi that his spirit was with him when he sinned.

When this spirit influences people, it will cause them to sell out their leaders as well as their own soul. It is a conniving and lying spirit. This spirit is very close to the one on Judas Iscariot.

Gehazi was the assistant minister to the number one ministry of his day. He could have easily inherited Elisha's mantle just like Elisha inherited Elijah's. Instead he gave it all up to cheat and seek self-gain. He became a leper, he died a leper, and his children were all leprous. Wow!

If you allow this spirit to speak to you, influence you, or indoctrinate you, then you also will become a self-seeker, liar, and conniver. You will go for the money or any other opportunity that the prophet turns down. You will be convinced that it's the only way to get ahead and that God isn't moving on your behalf. "After all, the prophet didn't want it. Why should I let it go to waste?"

The Spirit of Gehazi
Summary

1. This evil spirit will cause you to be jealous of the attention that your leader/pastor gets from people that you feel you should get.

2. This spirit will influence you to sneak around the ministry and deal with things your own way even though you know how your pastor has dealt with them.

3. You will be willing to hide things from your Christian leaders and the brethren in order to be "blessed."

4. You will take every opportunity you can to deal with people on the side and get all you can from them.

5. This spirit will cause you to lie to people and misrepresent your leader/pastor.

6. This spirit will actually lead you to give up your entire ministry future for today's pleasures.

7. This spirit will cause you to judge the motives of your pastor.

8. This spirit will cause you to judge the manner in which your pastor deals with people and certain situations.

The Spirit of Gehazi
Quiz

Ask yourself these questions:

1. Do you ever feel like your Christian leader gets all the attention while you do all the work?

2. Are you ever jealous of the attention that your pastor gets?

3. Do you ever judge how your pastor handles different things, and do you think you could do it better?

4. Do you ever wonder why your Christian leader (pastor) turns down business opportunities or certain offerings?

5. Do you scavenge everything you can that your pastor turns down (meetings, money, favor with people, etc.)?

6. Do you wish you were "the prophet" instead of doing what God has given you to do?

7. Have you ever lost track of the fact that the Spirit of the Lord and the spirit of the prophet are always with you?

If you answered yes to any of these questions, you are in trouble with God. Fast, pray, and go for mature spiritual help from a reputable minister of the gospel of Christ.

CHAPTER 10
THE SPIRIT OF ANANIAS
AND SAPPHIRA

"Holding Back a Little for Yourself and Lying to the Holy Ghost"

BEWARE . . . This demon wants you to commit blasphemy of the Holy Spirit by not keeping your word to the church.

"Neither was there any among them that lacked: for as many as were possessors of lands or houses sold them, and brought the prices of the things that were sold,

And laid them down at the apostles' feet: and distribution was made unto every man according as he had need.

And Joses, who by the apostles was surnamed Barnabas, (which is, being interpreted, The son of consolation,) a Levite, and of the country of Cyprus,

Having land, sold it, and brought the money, and laid it at the apostles' feet."

Acts 4:34-37

*"But a certain man named **Ananias**, with **Sapphira** his wife, sold a possession,*

*And **kept back part of the price**, his wife also being privy to it, and brought a certain part, and laid it at the apostles' feet.*

*But Peter said, Ananias, **why hath Satan filled thine heart to lie to the Holy Ghost**, and to keep back part of the price of the land?*

*Whiles it remained, was it not thine own? and after it was sold, was it not in thine own power? **why hast thou conceived this thing in thine heart**? thou hast **not lied unto men, but unto God**.*

And Ananias hearing these words fell down, and gave up the ghost: and great fear came on all them that heard these things.

And the young men arose, wound him up, and carried him out, and buried him.

And it was about the space of three hours after, when his wife, not knowing what was done, came in.

And Peter answered unto her, Tell me whether ye sold the land for so much? And she said, Yea, for so much.

*Then Peter said unto her, **How is it that ye have agreed together to tempt the Spirit of the Lord**? behold, the feet of them which have buried thy husband are at the door, and shall carry thee out.*

Then fell she down straightway at his feet, and yielded up the ghost: and the young men came in, and found her dead, and, carrying her forth, buried her by her husband.

And great fear came upon all the church, and upon as many as heard these things."

Acts 5:1-11

This is another one of those stories that just doesn't make much sense—in the natural I mean. Sure I understand the principles here, but I don't understand why a man would cash in everything and risk his eternal state just for a profit for a season.

Ananias saw and heard how Barnabas had sold a piece of land and sowed the profit into the Kingdom. Maybe Ananias saw the attention that he got and wanted some of it for himself. Either way, he blew it big time.

Ananias was guilty of lying to the Holy Spirit, but you wouldn't have convinced him of that. He felt he was right with God even though he cheated the Church (the Lord's Body) and the preacher (the Lord's vessel).

Ananias's basic sin was that "he held back a little for himself." Wouldn't a person not tithing be guilty of this same thing? or a person who pledges something to the church work and then only pays a part? I think so.

Peter was the bishop of this particular local church, so when Ananias came in that day to pay his part, Peter looked in the records and confronted him. Many preachers are too intimidated to do this or they just don't know the finances of their ministry.

This spirit also caused Sapphira (Ananias's wife) to commit the same sin by being an accomplice to the sin. She was also confronted by Peter and was found in her sin. Read this whole chapter later and see that the whole church enjoyed great signs and miracles after this sin was revealed and dealt with.

This spirit will cause you to actually lie to the Holy Spirit. I suppose this is blasphemy of the Holy Spirit.

Ananias probably had a little contention with Peter and for some reason kept back a little of the pledge money for himself. However, Jesus interpreted it as lying to the Holy Spirit, not to Peter. Ananias died and Peter kept right on preaching. I guess it's clear whose side the Lord was on.

This spirit will influence you to blaspheme the Holy Spirit. It will convince you that the preacher is not a real man of God and that it doesn't matter how you deal with him. Surprise!

I know people, and so do you, who have sinned as bad as Ananias and maybe worse. You must pray for them desperately so they will repent before it is too late. Many of them have cheated on their pledges or walked away and not given anything at all towards it.

Bind this demon in Jesus' name, and keep it away from you and your spouse. Keep your word and pay your pledges, even if for some reason you no longer attend the church where you pledged.

Nothing is worth dying for, and certainly nothing is worth committing blasphemy of the Holy Spirit over.

The Spirit of Ananias and Sapphira
Summary

1. This spirit will cause you to hold back a little for yourself.

2. This spirit will cause you to lie to your pastors and ultimately lie to the Holy Spirit.

3. This spirit will cause you to renege on your verbal commitments to the house of the Lord.

4. You will want to do right but will always cheat a little somewhere.

5. You will actually think it is okay to not keep your word with the preacher and the church you attend or the one you just left.

6. This spirit wants to eventually lead you to blasphemy of the Holy Spirit.

7. Your whole family will be sucked into this activity and end up paying the whole price with you.

The Spirit of Ananias and Sapphira
Quiz

Ask yourself these questions:

1. Do you ever keep back something for yourself that you promised God?

2. Do you ever only keep part of your promises and pledges to God and the church you attend?

3. Do you ever think it is okay with God that you treat your pastor with disrespect?

4. Do you ever feel like you got away with doing partial instead of doing all?

5. Do you ever involve your family in the wrongs that you do or that you allow?

6. Do you ever pretend in church or act like you are in good standing when you know in your heart that you are not?

7. Has this spirit already caused you to do things that you haven't repented of and repaired yet?

If you answered yes to any of these questions, you are in trouble with God. Fast, pray, and go for mature spiritual help from a reputable minister of the gospel of Christ.

CHAPTER 11
THE SPIRIT OF THE RICH
YOUNG RULER

"Interested but Not Hungry"

BEWARE . . . This spirit will tell you all kinds of reasons why you should not give up anything to follow Jesus. You will walk away holding its hand.

*"And, behold, one came and said unto him, Good Master, **what good thing shall I do, that I may have eternal life**?*

And he said unto him, Why callest thou me good? there is none good but one, that is, God: but if thou wilt enter into life, keep the commandments.

He saith unto him, Which? Jesus said, Thou shalt do no murder, Thou shalt not commit adultery, Thou shalt not steal, Thou shalt not bear false witness,

Honour thy father and thy mother: and, Thou shalt love thy neighbour as thyself.

*The young man saith unto him, **All these things have I kept from my youth up**: what lack I yet?*

*Jesus said unto him, If thou wilt be perfect, go and **sell that thou hast, and give to the poor, and thou***

*shalt have treasure in heaven: and come and follow
me.*

*But when the young man heard that saying, **he went
away sorrowful**: for he had great possessions."*

Matthew 19:16-22

*"And when he was gone forth into the way, there
came one running, and kneeled to him, and asked
him, Good Master, **what shall I do that I may inherit
eternal life**?*

*And Jesus said unto him, Why callest thou me good?
there is none good but one, that is, God.*

*Thou knowest the commandments, Do not commit
adultery, Do not kill, Do not steal, Do not bear false
witness, Defraud not, Honour thy father and mother.*

*And he answered and said unto him, Master, **all these
have I observed from my youth**.*

*Then Jesus beholding him loved him, and said unto
him, **One thing thou lackest**: go thy way, sell whatso-
ever thou hast, and give to the poor, and thou shalt
have treasure in heaven: and come, take up the cross,
and follow me.*

*And **he was sad at that saying, and went away
grieved**: for he had great possessions."*

Mark 10:17-22

*"And **a certain ruler asked** him, saying, Good Master,
what shall I do to inherit eternal life?*

*And Jesus said unto him, Why callest thou me good?
none is good, save one, that is, God.*

*Thou knowest the commandments, Do not commit
adultery, Do not kill, Do not steal, Do not bear false*

witness, Honour thy father and thy mother.

And he said, All these have I kept from my youth up.

Now when Jesus heard these things, he said unto him, **Yet lackest thou one thing***: sell all that thou hast, and distribute unto the poor, and thou shalt have treasure in heaven: and come, follow me.*

And when he heard this, **he was very sorrowful***: for he was very rich.*

And when Jesus saw that he was very sorrowful, he said, How hardly shall they that have riches enter into the kingdom of God!"

Luke 18:18-24

This rich young ruler was interested in Jesus and the kingdom of Heaven but would not pay the price. He knew to pay the price and could have but chose not to. This reminds me of many Christians today. They all are very interested and ask all the right questions but will not pay what it costs to walk with Jesus.

This young man knew to live right. When Jesus told him to do all the ten commandments, he said that he did and that he learned to as a youth. This is not what you would call a bad guy. His sin was that he was interested but not hungry.

Many people who are being influenced by this spirit will live a religious life but not a Christian one. They will keep all the commandments of convenience, but when there is personal sacrifice involved that requires faith, they grieve and walk away. I'll bet right now that this young man wishes to God that he would have given up money and possessions in order to follow Christ.

Jesus never told the man that he could do both. He made him choose between the world's riches and the kingdom of God. They just don't mix.

If you fellowship with this spirit, you will easily get fooled into thinking that your few religious acts of obedience will be enough to get you accepted in His sight or that you can serve Him anyway you want to. You must serve Jesus exactly how He says, not the way you want to.

You must be hungry enough to tell this mammon spirit to release you and chase after Jesus Christ. You see, many people make the "grave" mistake of thinking that you can go to Heaven without following Jesus. Heaven above depends entirely on your walk with Him in this life.

The other disciples immediately left their nets and followed after Him. This man wanted to add the net of Christianity to the many other nets he had. It won't work!

The Spirit of the Rich Young Ruler
Summary

1. This spirit will cause you to be influenced by money and possessions.

2. This spirit will influence you to hold loosely the things of God while tightening your grip on your prosperity.

3. You will be more than willing to give up your church ministry for overtime on the job.

4. You will be more than willing to relocate to a new region for the sake of pay raise even though you are not sure there is a good church there for your family.

5. It will bother you when the pastor takes serious offerings and puts a demand on you to help financially.

6. This spirit will cause you to abandon post in the kingdom of God in order to recreate or vacate.

7. This spirit will cause you to dilute God's prosperity to mere financial possessions.

8. This spirit will eventually lead you away from serving God and sink you in the world of greed and self-promotion.

The Spirit of the Rich Young Ruler
Quiz

Ask yourself these questions:

1. Does prosperity mean nothing to you but material gain?

2. Are you willing to trade your church worship times for your job?

3. Are you willing to relocate with your job future in mind even before you search out a new church in that region?

4. Are you ever worried that you are giving too much to the work of the Lord?

5. Do you ever feel that serving Jesus is going to cost you everything?

6. Do your job and your income mean more to you than your outcome?

7. Do you influence your family more to get ahead than you do to get close to God?

8. Do your hobbies and crafts and sports draw you away from His house more than occasionally?

If you answered yes to any of these questions, you are in trouble with God. Fast, pray, and go for mature spiritual help from a reputable minister of the gospel of Christ.

CHAPTER 12
THE SPIRIT OF ALEXANDER

"The Vicious Assaulting Spirit"

**BEWARE . . . This demon will convince you
to viciously assault Jesus' ministry. You will yell "abuse"
and accuse leaders falsely.**

"Holding faith, and a good conscience; which some having put away concerning faith have made ship-wreck:

Of whom is Hymenaeus and Alexander; whom I have delivered unto Satan, that they may learn not to blaspheme."

1 Timothy 1:19-20

*"**Alexander** the coppersmith did me much evil: the Lord reward him according to his works:*

Of whom be thou ware also; for he hath greatly withstood our words."

2 Timothy 4:14-15

There were some men whom the early apostles had little if anything good to say about. Alexander was one of these ill-fated men. For some reason he thought he could get away with persecuting and harming the ministry of Jesus Christ.

Paul eventually turned men like this over to satan for the destruction of the flesh so that if there was any chance at all that they may be saved, they would be. The eternal soul is much more important than the body we live in.

Paul was very bold and outspoken about this man who did his ministry harm. He didn't even say he forgave him. He said, "May the Lord reward him according to his deeds." This Alexander resisted the words of the man of God and withstood them. This is a little bit more severe than simply disagreeing with them.

I know people whom this spirit has gotten upon. They seem to be propelled to resist the ministry and forcefully stop it. They actually withstand the Word that is preached and normally cry "abuse" or say that the preacher is controlling.

Notice that Alexander found a friend to run with and to work with against the ministry. Today people go to private prayer meetings and—quote/unquote—Bible studies to get free from their local church and their pastor. They actually have exit counselors to teach people how to get free from church. It seems as though these anti-church, anti-pastor Christians yelling "abuse" and "spirit of control" are themselves under this spirit that was on Alexander.

> *"Alexander the coppersmith has done me much harm.* ***The Lord will punish him,***
>
> ***but be careful of him, for he fought against everything we said."***
>
> 2 Timothy 4:14-15 (TLB)

75

The Spirit of Alexander
Summary

1.   This demon will turn you against your Christian leaders.

2.   This spirit will convince you that your Christian leaders are your problem in life.

3.   This spirit will cause you to not only betray your pastor and your local church family but to do it viciously.

4.   This spirit will cause you to damage the kingdom of God and those in it, and all the time you will think you are doing God a favor.

5.   This spirit will drive you to split the church and slander your preacher.

6.   You will do the kingdom of God much harm, and a lot of it will be beyond repair.

7.   This spirit will eventually lead you to assault the church and its leaders until you have brought yourself under much condemnation.

The Spirit of Alexander
Quiz

Ask yourself these questions:

1. Do you ever think that you can speak against your brethren with the permission of God?

2. Do you ever feel like you are the only one in the whole group that is right?

3. Do you ever try to convince others in your church that you are the "right" one.

4. Do you maliciously slander your Christian leaders?

5. Do you ever do anything that would cause anybody to abandon their church or accuse their pastors?

6. Do you ever lead or attend fellowships or Bible studies that spend their time defaming or disassembling other ministries in any way?

7. Do you feel inner anger or resentment that Christians have done you wrong or that pastors are at fault for "your" activities and misbehaviors?

If you answered yes to any of these questions, you are in trouble with God. Fast, pray, and go for mature spiritual help from a reputable minister of the gospel of Christ.

CHAPTER 13
THREE REVELATIONS

These were given to me a few months apart and refer to the satanic and worldly attack against the Lord's Church and His leaders.

PEOPLE LEAVING THE MINISTRY

Early in the year 1986 the Lord began to show me the outcome of many ministries. I wasn't really asking Him for it, but I was very concerned about certain things, and this led me to prayer.

I began to receive phone calls from ministers who were leaving their pulpits and ministries. There were so many I had heard about and knew who were abandoning their post.

One day this revelation came to me by the Holy Spirit. I was presented this question: What was the major difference between Elijah and the prophets of Baal? Well, I answered right away that the difference was the god whom they were serving. Elijah served Jehovah. The other prophets served Baal. I heard the Lord tell me that this was a major difference but not the only major problem. The prophets of Baal wanted very much to be prophets. They wanted to be prophets so bad that they really didn't care whose prophets they were. Elijah hardly wanted to even be Jehovah's prophet.

As I meditated in this, I found the answer I'd been looking for and praying about. God was saying to me that there were many people who wanted to be in the fivefold ministry. They wanted to be in it so bad that they went off to Bible school or off on their own in order to preach and teach. Many of them were not called by God. They were not appointed by God; so when the flesh energy ran out, they puckered out! Many of these people today are falling left and right. They find themselves in big trouble, and their marriage and family are in trouble. They have used up all their own energy, and because God didn't call them to do what they are doing, He won't supply them with His energy. They will and are failing. They were seduced and deceived to give up everything for a ministry they were never called to fulfill.

Don't let it fret you that some are leaving the ministry or getting in trouble. Hook up to the "Elijahs" of God, and root yourself. God's men will bring you through. Everything will be alright if you stick with the real fruit-bearers.

A HYPODERMIC SYRINGE

In early 1986 the Spirit of the Lord revealed a powerful warning to me. I saw in the spirit a large hypodermic needle (the kind you would see in the doctor's office used to inoculate us when we need medicine or preventive boosters).

As I saw this, the Spirit of the Lord spoke to me that the body of Christ is being inoculated with what seems to be a worldly, fleshly serum. I saw that most of the Body did not realize this was happening. The maturity of this disease was like a slow, oozing death. Many Christians would cast off restraint and give themselves to the flesh, and many would even abandon the faith for worldly things or for the enjoyment of sin for a season.

In late 1986 and early 1987 I not only saw with my own eyes, but heard nationally, how many Christians, including ministers, were falling into temptation and didn't seem to have the ability to bounce back. I even saw some Christian people from my own church choose sin, pleasures, their jobs, wickedness, hardheartedness, and gossip over Kingdom principles.

(This is so real as I write this book. It is awesome to think about the eternal results of people's lives who fall for sin.)

THE CHARCOAL-COLORED, WITHERED HAND

In 1987 (the very early part of the year), I saw a vision of a man-like, yet creature-like, hand and forearm. It was as though the hand and forearm were skinny and hairy. It had been in a fire, and it was all withered and charcoal-colored, and the hair was singed and matted to the flesh. I saw at the end of the fingers a horn-like nail or claw sticking out. This hand came through the door of my church and made a curved swoop through the sanctuary. It didn't collect people in mass, but it did snare and hook a select few. It was as though these nail-like claws had a person stuck on each one. It began to withdraw itself from the sanctuary. As it moved toward the door it had entered, dragging these people with it, I thought to myself that I would just rebuke it in Jesus' name and that would be the end of it. But as I began to do this, I noticed that not one person who was stuck on any finger was struggling at all to get off. There was little movement and no screaming, rebuking, or wrestling going on. It was then that the Lord spoke to me and showed me that some people have given themselves over to satan and his devices, and they were more than ready to leave and break fellowship.

This saddened me, and I know that it wasn't only for my church. It was for the whole body of Christ. Today I see many people actually being dragged out of the church to serve the world and the devil, and they seem so willing. They leave, blaming the preacher or the other believers. Guard yourself. Don't sell out!

CONCLUSION

I hope you enjoyed this book, and I pray God opened your eyes to many things. I also hope you will meditate even more in the scriptures that are listed in this book. Your Bible is the key to a successful life. Try to read it every day and discover the principles we are to live by.

I pray for you that you will have a very long, very satisfying life serving our Lord and Savior.

Keep yourself clean, and do your very best to live uprightly.

Beware of your enemy, satan, and his schemes and plans to ruin your life.

God bless you.

A PRAYER FOR YOU

My prayer for you is:

". . . grant unto thy servants, that with all boldness they may speak thy word,

By stretching forth thine hand to heal; and that signs and wonders may be done by the name of thy holy child Jesus."

Acts 4:29-30

Heavenly Father, I beseech You in Jesus' name, that You would cause each of us to grow in the character of our being. Help us to be more pleasing to You than we ever have been. Help us to speak boldly yet in season. Help us to tell the truth and be what You want us to be.

Dear Lord, please melt away our facades, and help us to stop playing games. Help each of us to see the kingdom of God as the priority and not our own kingdom.

We are going to have backbone, Lord, in our servant-hood to You and our witness to the world.

We love You, Lord. Thank You for answering this prayer, Sir!

PRAYER OF SALVATION

YOU CAN BE SAVED
FROM ETERNAL DAMNATION!

Get God's help now, in this life. All you have to do is humble your heart, believe in Christ's work at Calvary for you, and pray the following prayer:

Dear Heavenly Father,

I know that I have sinned and fallen short of Your expectations of me. I have come to realize that I cannot run my own life. I do not want to continue the way I've been living, neither do I want to face an eternity of torment and damnation.

I know that the wages of sin is death, but I can be spared from this through the gift of the Lord Jesus Christ. I believe that He died for me, and I receive His provision now. I will not be ashamed of Him, and I will tell all my friends and family members that I have made this wonderful decision.

Dear Lord Jesus,

Come into my heart now and live in me and be my Savior, Master, and Lord. I will do my very best to chase after You and to learn Your ways by submitting to a pastor, reading my Bible, going to a church that preaches about You, and keeping sin out of my life.

I also ask You to give me the power to be healed from any sickness and disease and to deliver me from those things that have me bound.

I love You and thank You for having me, and I am eagerly looking forward to a long, beautiful relationship with You.

Books by Mark T. Barclay

Avoiding the Pitfalls of Familiarity

This book is a scriptural study on the most devastating sin in the body of Christ today. It includes four of life's examples of the sin of familiarity, five Bible examples, and three examples we may find in the local church. The last chapter tells how we can fight this sin and even what to do if we've blown it. This is information every believer, as well as every leader, must have!

Building a Supernatural Church

A guide to pioneering, organizing, and establishing a new local church. This is a fast-reading, simple, instructional guide to leaders and helps people who are working together to build the Church.

Enduring Hardness

God has called His Church an army and the believers, soldiers. It is mandatory that all Christians endure hardness as good soldiers of Jesus Christ. This book will help build more backbone in you.

How to Always Reap a Harvest

In this book Brother Barclay explains the principles that make believers successful and fruitful. It shows you how to live a better life and become far more productive and enjoy a full harvest.

How to Avoid Shipwreck

This book explains what a shipwrecked faith is, identifies who is headed that way and the deception some Christians fall into. It gives four great anchors of the soul which will cause stability in the most treacherous of life's storms.

How to Relate to Your Pastor

It is very important in these last days that God's people understand the office of pastor. As we put into practice these principles, the Church will grow in numbers and also increase its vision for the world.

How to Survive a Betrayal

Often the most difficult thing to deal with concerning betrayal is the fact that it almost always comes from the people you love, trust, or respect. This amazing book will help you press on, recover, and once again become productive when a betrayal strikes your heart.

Improving Your Performance

Brother Barclay covers the spectrum of important church issues, including leadership versus lordship, consistency, honesty, humility, love, and much more. He speaks first to the pastors and then to the church on each issue. It's a great unity builder for every church!

One Day–Thought–Year (By Vickie L. Barclay)
A Daily Devotional for Women of Righteousness

This book is filled with daily verses and real life stories to inspire and encourage you. May the Lord visit you each and every day, and may you draw closer to Him than you have ever been before. As your relationship with Him deepens, may it empower you to accomplish the ultimate goal of a Christian—to win souls and disciple them. That is my desire, and that is the heart behind writing this book.

Preachers of Righteousness

This is not a book for pulpiteers or reverends only but for all of us. It reveals the real ministry style of Jesus Christ and the sold-out commitment of His followers—the most powerful, awesome force on the face of the earth.

Sheep, Goats, Wolves

A scriptural yet practical explanation of human behavior in our local churches and how church leaders and members can deal with each other. You will especially enjoy the tests that are in the back of this book.

Six Ways to Check Your Leadings

It seems that staying in the main flow of Jesus is one of the most difficult things for believers to do, including some preachers. Many people border on mysticism and a world of fantasy. God is not a goofy god. He doesn't intend for His people to be goofy either. This book reveals the six most valuable New Testament ways to live in accuracy and stay perfectly on course. This book is a must for living in these last days.

The Making of a Man of God

In this book you'll find some of the greatest, yet simplest, insights to becoming a man or woman of God and to launching your ministry with accuracy and credibility. The longevity of your ministry will be enhanced by the truths herein. You will learn the difference between being a convert, an epistle, a disciple, and a minister.

The Real Truth About Tithing

With the extremely fast lifestyles of these last days, it leaves little time to thoroughly study God's Word. When you finish this book, you will be fully equipped and informed to tithe properly and accurately. All of your tithing questions should be answered. Your life will never be the same.

The Remnant Church

God has always had a people and will always have a people. Brother Barclay speaks of the upcoming revival and how we can be those who are alive and remain when our Master returns.

The Sin of Lawlessness

Jesus warned us that in the last days the sin of lawlessness would increase. It causes people to challenge those in authority, and it ultimately hurts people. This is a hard-hitting book that exposes the excuses troubled people use to attack all kinds of leadership. It includes an extensive explanation and characteristics of what the "spots and wrinkles" are in the Body of Christ, as well as Bible antidotes. The final chapter is a stern warning to guard yourself from harmful situations.

Things You Need for the Day Ahead

This book was written to alert everyone (sinner and saint) to the coming perils, calamities, and filth that human power will not be able to overcome. The times will be extremely dangerous and eternally damning. That's why I wrote this simple-reading, hard-hitting book. Those who cling to truth and the Lord Jesus Christ will make it—some as survivors and some as conquerors. They will endure to the end.

Walking With God

A handbook for the Spirit-filled life, this book is sure to stir you on in pursuing more of the things of the Spirit. It also makes a great gift for those who don't understand the Spirit-filled life, giving thorough explanation, mixed with real experience, regarding the following topics: The Ministry of the Holy Spirit; The Holy Spirit in Action; No Mere Man; Holy Spirit Baptism; The Anointing; Led by the Spirit; How to Check Your Leadings; The Eyes of Your Spirit; The Armor of God; The Fruit of the Spirit; The Gifts of God; How to Develop in the Gifts; On Fire for God; Making the Holy Spirit Your Best Friend!

Warring Mental Warfare

Every person is made up of body, soul, and spirit and fights battles on each of these three fronts. The war against your soul (made up of your mind, will, and emotions) is real and as lethal as spiritual and natural enemies. This book will help you identify, war against, and defeat the enemies of your soul. Learn to quit coping with depression, anxiety, fear, and other hurts, and begin conquering those things now!

What About Death?

In this book, Brother Barclay deals with the enemy (death) and how to overcome it. He also explains what the Bible says about life after death. Many people have no real Bible knowledge on this subject and therefore are unsure about it all the days of their lives.